I Will Die

A CREATIVE JOURNAL
FOR MORTALS

by Jessica Featherly

DEEP DOWN PRESS

Cover by Jessica Featherly

Printed in the United States of America

Published by
DEEP DOWN PRESS

www.deepdownpress.com

BEING MORTAL MEANS WE HAVE AN EXPIRATION DATE.
LIFE DOES NOT LAST. LIFE IS FINITE, TRANSIENT, PASSING.
THAT'S WHY IT IS BEAUTIFUL AND HAS MEANING.

DEATH IS INESCAPABLE AND IMMINENT –
FOR ME, FOR YOU, FOR THOSE YOU LOVE.
FOR EVERY ONE OF US, 100% OF THE TIME.
THIS IS THE SITUATION WE, AS MORTALS, ARE IN.
RESISTANCE IS FUTILE.

THIS CREATIVITY JOURNAL IS FILLED WITH
DEEP AND SOMETIMES PLAYFUL
CREATIVE WRITING AND ARTISTIC PROMPTS,
DESIGNED TO HELP YOU EXPLORE YOUR OWN EMOTIONS
AND BELIEFS ABOUT DEATH AND DYING,
AND HOW THEY AFFECT THE WAY YOU LIVE.
LOOK YOUR MORTALITY IN THE FACE,
CONTEMPLATE THE DREAD & WONDER OF IT,
AND EVERYTHING ABOUT LIFE BECOMES
ALL THE MORE PRECIOUS AND MEANINGFUL.

LET THE JOURNEY BEGIN…

WRITE 'I WILL DIE' IN THE SPACE BELOW.
UNDERLINE IT, SIGN AND DATE IT.

THERE'S NO WAY AROUND IT, EVERYONE WILL SOMEDAY DIE. AND SO WILL YOU.

DO YOU OFTEN THINK ABOUT DEATH *AND* DYING?
WHY OR WHY NOT?

WRITE DOWN ALL THE EUPHEMISMS YOU CAN THINK OF
THAT PEOPLE USE FOR 'DEATH':

WHY CAN'T (OR WON'T) PEOPLE JUST SAY
'HE DIED' OR 'SHE IS DEAD'?

DO YOU THINK MORE ABOUT YOUR OWN DEATH
OR ABOUT THE DEATH OF OTHERS?

WHAT DOES DEATH LOOK LIKE?
DRAW SOME THINGS:

AT WHAT TIMES & PLACES DO YOU FEAR DEATH
THE MOST?

WHAT IF YOU COULD LIVE FOREVER?

WOULD YOU WANT TO?

HOW WOULD YOUR LIFE BE DIFFERENT THAN IT IS NOW?

10 THINGS YOU WOULD DO IF YOU KNEW YOU
COULD NOT DIE.

DO YOU THINK DEATH IS NATURAL OR UN-NATURAL?
WHY?

WHAT IS THE DIFFERENCE BETWEEN A
'GOOD DEATH' AND A 'BAD DEATH'?

WHERE WOULD YOU LIKE TO BE AT THE TIME YOU DIE,
AND WHAT WOULD YOU BE DOING?

DOES LOVE END AT DEATH?

WHAT GOALS DO YOU DEFINITELY WANT TO ACHIEVE BEFORE YOU DIE?

WOULD YOU RATHER DIE UNEXPECTEDLY,
OR KNOW THAT IT WAS IMMINENT? WHY?

LIST FIVE WAYS YOU WOULD PREFER TO DIE:

WRITE DOWN THE WORST WAYS YOU CAN THINK OF
TO DIE:

HAVE YOU EVER HAD AN EXPERIENCE WHERE YOU THOUGHT YOU MIGHT DIE?

WHAT HAPPENED & HOW DID IT MAKE YOU FEEL?

WHAT THOUGHTS DO YOU THINK YOU WILL HAVE
WHEN YOU KNOW YOU ARE DYING?

MY BIGGEST FEARS ABOUT DYING
(CHECK ALL THAT APPLY):

PEOPLE I LOVE DYING BEFORE I DO

FEAR I WILL MISS OUT

DYING ALONE AND UNLOVED

THAT OTHERS WILL BLAME ME FOR MY OWN DEATH

THAT I WON'T BE REMEMBERED

THAT I HAVE NO LEGACY

THAT I'M LEAVING A HUGE MESS BEHIND

I'LL MISS MY CHILDREN GROWING UP

IT WILL HURT

I WON'T BE ABLE TO CATCH MY BREATH

SUFFERING

MY LIFE WILL HAVE BEEN POINTLESS

NOT KNOWING WHAT COMES NEXT

NOT HAVING LIVED AS FULLY AS I WANT

THAT I'LL WISH I COULD HAVE DONE IT SOONER

THAT IT WON'T HAPPEN QUICKLY

THAT I WON'T GET INTO HEAVEN

THAT I'LL HAVE FORGOTTEN TO LOCK THE FRONT DOOR

THAT IT WILL BREAK MY FAMILY'S HEARTS

BEING A BURDEN ON OTHERS

MY PRIDE WILL BE HURT

THE INDIGNITY OF BEING A CORPSE

BEING UNPREPARED

THAT MY PETS WON'T BE TAKEN CARE OF

THAT MY FAMILY WILL SEE EVERYTHING ON MY HARD DRIVE

LOSING CONTROL

MY "TO DO" LIST WON'T GET DONE

THE POSSIBILITY THAT MY CONSCIOUSNESS MIGHT LINGER

LOOKING REALLY AWFUL

LOSING MY MIND

MY DEATH WILL BE STUPID

MY CHERISHED MEMORIES WILL DIE WITH ME

THAT I DIDN'T TO MORE WITH THE TIME I HAD

BEING FORGOTTEN

DARKNESS

ANNIHILATION

MY END OF LIFE WISHES WON'T BE RESPECTED

FEAR OF THE UNKNOWN

I WILL BE NO MORE

LEAVING BEHIND UNFINISHED BUSINESS

OTHER FEARS YOU HAVE ABOUT DYING:

DO YOU EVER THINK ABOUT SUICIDE? WHY OR WHY NOT?

HOW DOES SUICIDE AFFECT THOSE LEFT BEHIND?

Do you have the right to choose how you will die?

WHAT WOULD YOU DO OR SAY TO SOMEONE
WHO WANTED TO COMMIT SUICIDE?

LIST THE WAYS YOU DENY THE REALITY
THAT YOU DEFINITELY ARE GOING TO DIE:

IS DEATH AN END OR A BEGINNING?
ARRIVING AT A DESTINATION OR THE START OF
A JOURNEY?

WHAT ARE SOME NOT-SO-SCARY THINGS ABOUT DYING,
THAT DON'T REALLY BOTHER YOU:

REASONS WHY IT IS GOOD TO BE MORTAL,
INSTEAD OF LIVING FOREVER:

WHAT PREPARATIONS HAVE YOU MADE
FOR YOUR OWN DEATH?

WOULD YOU WANT TO DONATE YOUR ORGANS?
WHICH ONES?

WHAT STEPS SHOULD YOU TAKE TO MAKE SURE THIS COULD HAPPEN?

WOULD YOU WANT TO BE EMBALMED?
WHY OR WHY NOT?

WOULD YOU DONATE YOUR BODY TO SCIENCE?
WHAT WOULD YOU LIKE IT TO BE USED FOR?

TEN THINGS YOU WOULD REALLY LIKE TO TAKE WITH YOU
WHEN YOU DIE:

THINGS AND PLACES YOU WILL MISS THE MOST
WHEN YOU DIE:

QUESTIONS YOU'D LIKE ANSWERS TO BEFORE YOU DIE:

WHAT ARE SOME OF YOUR MOST CHERISHED POSSESSIONS, AND WHO DO YOU WANT TO HAVE THEM AFTER YOU DIE?

WHAT WILL HAPPEN TO ALL YOUR OTHER STUFF
WHEN YOU ARE GONE?

SOME BELIEVE THAT THINKING OR TALKING ABOUT DEATH
IS TABOO, BECAUSE THAT SOMEHOW INVOKES IT.
WHAT DO YOU THINK?

LIST EVERYTHING YOU'D LIKE TO EAT FOR YOUR LAST MEAL:

DESCRIBE YOUR IDEAL FINAL DAY:

WHAT DO YOU REGRET THE MOST ABOUT
SOMEONE YOU LOVE DYING?

WHAT DO YOU BELIEVE YOU WILL REGRET THE MOST
WHEN YOU ARE DYING?

DO YOU HAVE ANY MEMORIES OF DEATH
FROM YOUR CHILDHOOD?

THINGS YOU NEED TO LET GO OF BEFORE YOU DIE:

WHAT YOU WOULD LIKE TO BE WEARING WHEN YOU DIE:

WHAT WOULD YOU LIKE YOUR FINAL
TEXT, TWEET OR FACEBOOK POST TO BE?

WHO WOULD YOU LIKE TO BE WITH YOU WHEN YOU DIE? WHY?

WHAT WOULD YOU LIKE YOUR LAST WORDS TO BE?

THINGS THAT ARE ALL THE MORE PRECIOUS TO YOU
BECAUSE THEY DO NOT LAST:

WHAT ACTIVITIES MAKE YOU FEEL THE MOST ALIVE?

WHAT ACTIVITIES MAKE YOU FEEL THE MOST DEAD?

IF YOU KNEW YOU HAD ONLY ONE YEAR LEFT TO LIVE,
HOW WOULD YOU SPEND YOUR TIME DIFFERENTLY?

IF YOU WERE DYING TODAY,
WHAT WOULD YOUR FINAL WISH BE?

DO YOU EVER HAVE DREAMS ABOUT DYING?

IF SOMEONE YOU LOVED WAS ABOUT TO DIE BUT
DIDN'T KNOW, WOULD YOU TELL THEM?

WHAT DO YOU THINK WILL HAPPEN
TO YOUR BODY AFTER YOU DIE?

WHAT DO YOU THINK HAPPENS TO YOUR SPIRIT
AFTER YOU HAVE DIED?

IN WHAT WAYS DOES SPIRIT 'YOU' DIFFER FROM THE FLESH & BLOOD 'YOU'?

THINGS YOU WANT TO DO IN YOUR AFTERLIFE:

Do you feel you need forgiveness before you die?

IS THERE SOMEONE YOU NEED TO FORGIVE
BEFORE YOU DIE?

WOULD YOU WANT TO KNOW THE EXACT DATE OF YOUR DEATH? WHY OR WHY NOT?

WHAT IS THE BEST THING ABOUT A SLOW DEATH?
THE WORST THING?

WHAT IS THE BEST THING ABOUT A QUICK DEATH?
THE WORST THING?

WHAT MAKES YOU MOST UNCOMFORTABLE WHEN
YOU ARE AROUND SOMEONE WHO IS DYING?

WHAT WOULD YOU WANT TO SAY TO A FRIEND WHO IS
FACING DEATH? HOW WOULD YOU IDEALLY WISH
TO SPEND TIME WITH THEM?

OF FRIENDS AND FAMILY WHO HAVE DIED,
WHO DO YOU MISS THE MOST?

OF THE PEOPLE YOU KNOW NOW,
WHO WILL YOU MISS THE MOST WHEN THEY DIE?

HOW AFRAID ARE YOU OF LOSING A FRIEND OR FAMILY MEMBER? WHAT FRIGHTENS YOU THE MOST ABOUT THEIR DYING?

HOW HAS THE DEATH OF A LOVED ONE CHANGED YOU?

IS THERE ANYONE OR ANY CAUSE
YOU WOULD WILLINGLY DIE FOR?

HOW DO YOU FEEL WHEN SOMEONE YOU LOVE DIES
AND YOU WEREN'T ABLE TO SEE THEM ONE LAST TIME?
WHAT WOULD YOU LIKE TO SAY TO THEM?

Do you feel you've been able to truly grieve when someone close to you has died?

HAVE YOU FELT PRESSURE FROM OTHER PEOPLE TO DEAL
WITH GRIEF AND LOSS IN A SPECIFIC WAY?
DO YOU FEEL IS THERE A 'RIGHT' WAY
OR A 'WRONG' WAY TO GRIEVE?

WHAT GIVES YOU THE MOST COMFORT AND SOLACE
WHEN YOU ARE GRIEVING?

HAVE YOU EVER BEEN WITH SOMEONE WHEN THEY TOOK THEIR LAST BREATH?

DO YOU THINK DIFFERENTLY ABOUT DEATH THAN YOUR CLOSE FRIENDS & FAMILY DO? HOW SO?

WHAT DO YOU WISH YOU COULD SAY TO YOUR FAMILY
ABOUT DEATH?

WHO CAN YOU TALK TO ABOUT DEATH AND DYING?

WHAT WAYS DO YOU LIKE TO REMEMBER
SOMEONE WHO HAS DIED?

WHAT ARE SOME OF YOUR FAVORITE BOOKS AND MOVIES ABOUT DYING, AND WHY?

DRAW A PICTURE REPRESENTING 'GRIEF'.

THE NAMES OF YOUR PETS THAT HAVE DIED:

HOW DID THEIR DEATHS AFFECT YOU?

DO YOU THINK OF DEATH AS A FRIEND
OR AS AN ENEMY - OR BOTH?

WRITE YOUR OBITUARY
AS YOU'D LIKE IT TO BE IN THE NEWSPAPER:

WHICH OF THE FOLLOWING DO YOU FEEL YOUR FUNERAL IS FOR:

TO COMFORT MY FAMILY & LOVED ONES
SO OTHERS WILL KNOW I DIED
TO ACKNOWLEDGE I WAS HERE
SO OTHERS WILL FEEL THE LOSS OF ME
TO GIVE CLOSURE
ONE MORE TIME TO SAY GOODBYE
CELEBRATION OF MY LIFE
TO MOURN MY DEATH
TO SHOW RESPECT
TO REMIND OTHERS THAT THEY WILL DIE TOO
IT IS A FORMALITY
TO MANAGE THE PRACTICAL DETAILS OF MY BURIAL
I'M NOT HAVING ONE

OTHER:

WHO DO YOU WANT TO DRESS AND BATHE YOU WHEN YOU DIE?

WHAT CLOTHING DO YOU WANT TO BE BURIED OR CREMATED IN?

MY BEST OUTFIT
NOTHING SPECIAL
PAJAMAS
SWEATS
A SHROUD
THE BLOOD OF MY ENEMIES
JEANS & T-SHIRT
A COSTUME
NOTHING
OTHER:

WHAT OBJECTS WOULD YOU LIKE TO BE IN YOUR CASKET
WITH YOU?

WHAT ARE YOUR FEELINGS ABOUT FUNERALS
AND FUNERAL HOMES?

WOULD YOU PREFER TO BE BURIED OR CREMATED? WHY?

WHAT KIND OF FUNERAL OR CEREMONY
DO YOU WANT WHEN YOU DIE?

TOP 5 LOCATIONS WHERE YOU'D LIKE YOUR
FUNERAL OR MEMORIAL TO BE HELD:

TOP FIVE PLACES YOU WOULD LIKE TO BE BURIED OR
YOUR ASHES PLACED:

WHO WILL CARRY OUT YOUR LAST WISHES AND FUNERAL?

WHERE ARE YOUR WILL, IMPORTANT DOCUMENTS AND INSTRUCTIONS STORED? WHO KNOWS THIS?

WHAT SPECIFIC INSTRUCTIONS DO YOU WANT TO LEAVE
REGARDING YOUR FUNERAL, BURIAL OR CREMATION?

SONGS YOU WOULD LIKE PLAYED AT YOUR
FUNERAL OR MEMORIAL SERVICE:

WRITE A MESSAGE TO THOSE ATTENDING YOUR FUNERAL:

WHO YOU WOULD LIKE TO DO YOUR EULOGY
AND WHAT WOULD YOU LIKE THEM TO SAY
ABOUT YOU?

WHAT EPITAPH WOULD YOU LIKE ON YOUR TOMBSTONE?

A FEW DESIGNS FOR YOUR TOMBSTONE:

10 PEOPLE YOU HOPE WILL OUTLIVE YOU:

PEOPLE YOU WOULD LIKE TO OUTLIVE:

WHO WOULD YOU WANT TO REALLY MISS YOU
AFTER YOU DIE:

THINGS YOU WANT TO BE REMEMBERED FOR:

THINGS YOU DO NOT WANT TO BE REMEMBERED FOR:

DO YOU HAVE A SECRET HUNCH ABOUT HOW OR WHERE YOU WILL DIE?

IS DEATH SOMETHING TO BE RESISTED OR ACCEPTED?

DRAW FIVE THINGS SYMBOLIZING 'DEATH' TO YOU:

HOW OLD YOU WOULD LIKE TO BE BEFORE YOU DIE:

HOW MANY YEARS ARE LEFT TO YOU IF YOU LIVE TO THIS AGE:

DO YOU THINK YOU WILL LIVE THAT LONG?

WHAT TIME OF YEAR YOU WOULD LIKE TO DIE, AND WHY:

IF YOU COULD RETURN AFTER YOU DIE,
WHAT FORM WOULD YOU LIKE TO TAKE?

IS IT WRONG TO WANT TO DIE? WHY OR WHY NOT?

WHAT DO YOU THINK OF OUT-OF-BODY OR
NEAR DEATH EXPERIENCES?

WHAT HAPPENS TO TIME ONCE YOU ARE DEAD?

DESCRIBE THE PAIN OF LOSING A LOVED ONE.

ARE THE DEAD NEAR US OR FAR AWAY?

Do you want to be awake and aware as you die or would you rather be sedated and oblivious?

WHY DO YOU THINK PEOPLE OFTEN SEE DEPARTED
FAMILY MEMBERS WHEN THEY ARE CLOSE TO DEATH?

WHAT WILL LIFE BE LIKE FOR THOSE YOU'VE LEFT BEHIND
A YEAR AFTER YOU DIE?

5 YEARS AFTER YOU DIE?

10 YEARS AFTER YOU DIE?

COMPOSE A HAIKU ABOUT DEATH:

COPY A FAVORITE POEM ABOUT DEATH HERE:

WRITE DOWN SOME FAVORITE QUOTES ABOUT DEATH:

MORE QUOTES, VERSES OR QUESTIONS ABOUT DEATH:

HOW IMPORTANT IS 'YOUR LEGACY' TO YOU?
WHAT DO YOU WANT YOUR LEGACY TO BE?

WRITE LETTERS TO THOSE YOU LOVE
THAT ARE TO BE DELIVERED AFTER YOU DIE.

IS THINKING ABOUT DEATH DIFFICULT BECAUSE
IT FORCES US TO REALIZE HOW VERY LITTLE
CONTROL WE HAVE OVER OUR LIVES?

WHY IS 'CONTROL' SO ESSENTIAL TO US?

DRAW A PICTURE OF HOW YOU'LL LOOK
100 YEARS FROM NOW:

HOW CAN YOU PREPARE YOURSELF
FOR THE DEATHS OF THOSE YOU LOVE?

THINGS YOU CAN DO TO COME TO TERMS WITH
YOUR OWN MORTALITY:

HOW DOES THE INEVITABILITY OF YOUR DEATH
AFFECT THE WAY YOU LIVE TODAY?

SKETCHES, RANDOM THOUGHTS AND THINGS TO PONDER:

EVERYTHING COMES TO AN END.
AS SOON AS A THING BEGINS, IT STARTS FOR ITS END.
AS SOON AS A THING IS BORN, IT IS ON ITS WAY TO ITS DEATH.
THE PEOPLE WHO LIVED 7000 YEARS AGO
LOVED AND HATED, DANCED AND SANG,
AND DID JUST WHAT WE ARE DOING
AND NOW ONLY CRUMBLING RUINS OF THEIR GIANT TEMPLES
ARE LEFT TO TELL THE TALE.
THE LITTLE TROUBLES AND WORRIES WE HAVE TODAY
WILL ONLY BE A MEMORY THIS TIME NEXT YEAR.
A HUNDRED YEARS FROM NOW THERE WON'T BE A PERSON ALIVE
WHO IS HERE TODAY.
NOTHING IS AS IMPORTANT AS WE THINK IT IS.
THE POWER AND WEALTH THAT WE POSSESS TODAY
WILL PASS INTO OTHER HANDS.
THE LEAVES THAT FLUTTERED DOWN FROM THE TREES
THIS FALL WILL NEXT YEAR BE REPLACED BY OTHER LEAVES
WHO NEVER KNEW OF THEM OR WOULDN'T CARE.
LET US CHEER UP AND GET ALL THE JOY WE CAN
RIGHT NOW.

- R. F. OUTCAULT
1904.

Made in the USA
Las Vegas, NV
01 November 2024

10808207R00079